VITAL LIVING

sleep

for a calmer you

This edition published in 2019
By SJG Publishing, HP22 6NF, UK

Author: Becky Dickinson
Cover design: Milestone Creative
Contents design: Jo Ross, Double Fish Design Ltd

ISBN: 978-1-911517-85-6

Printed in China

10 9 8 7 6 5 4 3 2 1

contents

Introduction 5

Chapter 1. For the love of sleep 7

Chapter 2. Why do we sleep? 15

Chapter 3. Sleep and the brain 25

Chapter 4. Sleep and the body 33

Chapter 5. Beauty sleep and the beasts 45

Chapter 6. Defeating the beasts: how to improve your sleep 57

Chapter 7. Weird, wonderful and wise: the
Zzzz list of sleep hacks 77

There is a time for many words, and there is also a time for sleep.

HOMER

introduction

Few things in life make us feel better than a great night's sleep. Deep, peaceful sleep is that glorious state in which we switch off from the world and surrender to the subconscious. It is, perhaps, the defining act of escapism, the ultimate form of 'me-time'.

As day narrows into night, there is nothing better than climbing in to a warm, comfortable bed and closing our eyes. In an ideal world, we would simply turn out the light, hang up our worries and wake up eight hours later.

How blessed are
some people, whose
lives have no fears,
no dreads; to whom
sleep is a blessing that
comes nightly, and
brings nothing but
sweet dreams.

BRAM STOKER

CHAPTER 1

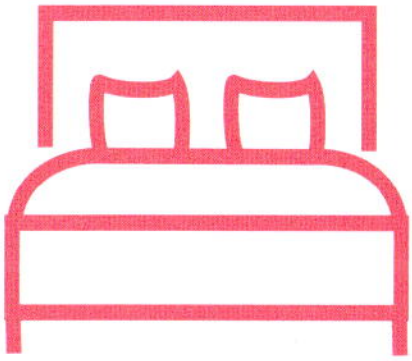

for the love of sleep

Contrary to outward appearances, sleep isn't a period of shutting down. Rather, it's a phase of intense activity. In the closing of our eyes and the unravelling of our mind, a window of opportunity opens, allowing the body to perform obligatory renovations and repairs; a nocturnal 'to do' list carried out under the shadow of darkness and the comfort of a duvet. It's this process of rest and repair that resets our bodies and brains, and enables us to get up morning after morning, refreshed, recharged and raring to go.

That's the theory anyway, or at least it would be if we could actually nod off. Unfortunately, for many of us, the perfect night's sleep is something we can only dream of – with the added irony that we're not actually dreaming. Stress, work, lifestyle, children, health, thoughts, anxieties and a whole host of other factors, all seek to sabotage our relationship with sleep, interfering with both the quality and quantity.

Whether it's a case of staying up late to 'get stuff done' because there aren't enough hours in the day, or an inability to 'switch off,' millions of us fall woefully short of the recommended seven to nine hours a night.

But sleep isn't a luxury or an indulgence, or even a choice. It's a basic, biological human need, as compelling and as sustaining as food, sex and water. Despite incredible advances in science and technology, we remain governed by the same primal drives as our ancestors. And while we could arguably live without sex for any given period of time (aside from the issue of reproduction), most of us start to crave sleep after just one night of abstinence.

Like hunger, sleep is governed by a deep internal force, and the longer we try to ignore it, the more powerful and demanding it becomes. In the same way as going without food creates an overwhelming desire to eat, going without sleep produces an all-consuming urge to close our eyes and nod off.

However weak-willed we are when it comes to dieting, it remains far easier to function on an empty stomach than it does on an empty quota of sleep; we can survive without food for forty days, and even manage without water for around three days – but try not going to bed for just a couple of nights and the consequences are almost intolerable. In fact, throughout history sleep deprivation has been used as a particularly insidious form of torture and interrogation.

Whether it's down to the occasional 'all-nighter' or a case of chronic insomnia, many of us are all too familiar – sometimes horribly so – with the effects of sleep deprivation. A one-off late or interrupted night is unlikely to cause any lasting damage and we can generally catch up the following night, but regular sleep deprivation leads to a heap of miserable repercussions.

From an overwhelming sense of fatigue, to feeling irritable and dazed, to feeling like you just can't face another human, let alone the world, the longer we go without sleep, the worse we feel. You could say it's like suffering from an almighty hangover, without actually having been to the party. And just as there is no real cure for a hangover, no amount of caffeine can undo the effects of too many late or sleepless nights.

Sleep is such an important part of life that we spend one-third of our lives in its embrace. That can seem like a colossal amount, especially when there are emails to answer, assignments to complete, dishwashers to load, social events to attend and TV dramas to watch. Yet we skimp on sleep at our peril. Because while there is still much mystery to uncover, one thing we do know is that we can't do without it. Sleep doesn't just make us feel better; it plays a vital role in keeping us alive and out of danger.

On the other hand, a lack of sleep leaves us feeling groggy, cross and generally subhuman. It impairs memory and cognitive function, making us more prone to error and lapses of concentration. Regular sleep deprivation can also have devastating implications for both physical and mental health, weakening the immune system and increasing the risk of numerous conditions, including obesity, diabetes, cancer, Alzheimer's and cardiovascular disease, as well as depression and other mood disorders.

In short, getting enough sleep is vital to our overall health and happiness, and we need to value it in the same way as we value other areas of well-being such as diet and exercise. Getting your eight hours a night is as important as getting your five-a-day. Yet in an increasingly fast-paced, competitive 21st century, sleep has become progressively harder to come by. Whether through a desire to stay awake, or the inability to switch off, millions of us simply aren't getting enough of it.

Fortunately, we are at last waking up to the fact that this won't do. Sleep is not something that we can simply cut back on, like gluten, or dairy. We need it like we need food, oxygen and water. What's more, getting enough sleep actually makes us more productive and more successful when we're awake.

The extreme discomfort that comes from not sleeping only serves to highlight its importance. It's as if the unbearable feelings that accompany a deficit of sleep are the body's way of telling us not to tamper with our biological clocks. Unfortunately, the punishing physical and mental symptoms of tiredness aren't always enough to ensure we to get more sleep.

As anyone prone to insomnia will appreciate, going to bed at a reasonable hour, even when preceded by a lavender-scented bath and a glass of warm milk, is sadly no guarantee of sleep success. The central and infinitely frustrating paradox of sleep is that the more we strive to achieve it, the harder it becomes to attain. Later, we'll discover how to escape this vicious cycle.

The good news is that knowledge brings change, and sleep is back in fashion. And just like changing the bedding or repositioning the furniture, you can transform the way you sleep. It might not happen overnight, but it will change your life. So seeing as you're already awake, why not continue reading to find out how?

Though sleep is called our best friend, it is a friend who often keeps us waiting!

JULES VERNE

did you know?

All mammals, birds and reptiles sleep. Other creatures like fish and amphibians seem to reduce their awareness without becoming unconscious.

Giraffes sleep for a mere 30 minutes a day, often in short bursts of five minutes at a time. Brown bats, on the other hand, sleep for almost 20 hours a day.

Horses, giraffes and elephants can all sleep standing up.

Some marine animals including whales and dolphins can literally sleep with half their brain at a time. This is called unihemispheric sleep. The other half of the brain remains alert.

The amount of time for which an animal sleeps is related to how much time it spends eating. Herbivores tend to sleep for less time than carnivores because they need to spend more time munching to get enough food.

In what is possibly the loveliest sleep fact of all time, otters hold hands when they sleep so that they don't drift apart.

Fatigue is the best pillow.

BENJAMIN FRANKLIN

CHAPTER 2

why do we sleep?

The trouble with sleep is that it's impossible to appreciate at the time of occurrence, for the simple reason that it's hard to enjoy something when you're not actually conscious.

Unlike indulging in a delicious slice of chocolate cake, the pleasure of sleep is only experienced in hindsight - in contrast to that slice of cake, which may just lead to feelings of regret. Trying to catch yourself sleeping is like trying to catch your own shadow; however close you get, there will always be that impassable line of separation. No sooner have you crossed it, than you're awake.

Since sleeping takes place outside the realms of our own immediate experience and provides no instant gratification, why do we need to sleep at all?

The obvious answer is we sleep because we get tired and because we feel rubbish when we don't.

But why hasn't evolution adapted to enable us to keep up with the demands of the 21st century? Why must we keep taking time out to do nothing? After all, when many of us lead such busy lives, it seems rather superfluous, gratuitous even, to spend eight hours out of every twenty-four in a state of apparent inactivity. But since going without sleep – either intentionally or otherwise – makes us feel utterly, universally horrendous, it must serve an important function. One thing we do know about sleep is that it's a basic biological necessity, as vital as breathing, drinking and eating. The final proof of this is that extreme sleep deprivation leads to certain death.

So in order to answer the question, 'why do we sleep?', we need to start by asking the question, 'what is sleep and what actually goes on?' On one level, sleep is simply the opposite of being awake. In slightly more scientific terms, it's usually defined as a reduction in physical activity and a decreased response to outside stimuli. This state is quickly reversible, meaning it's easy to wake up, unlike being in a coma, for example, or going into hibernation (if you happen to be a bear or a hedgehog).

And crucially, while it may look as if we are doing nothing at all, those eight hours (if you're lucky) of 'time out' provide the stage for a profound period of complex physiological and mental activity – which scientists are finally beginning to unravel.

Although it's hard to understand what goes on during sleep from the outside, it's possible to gain an inkling by looking at changes in brain activity using an EEG (electroencephalogram). When we are awake, the brain produces alpha and beta waves, but during sleep different patterns take over.

There are two basic types of sleep: rapid eye movement, or REM, and non-REM, which can be broken down into four different stages. One full sleep cycle is made up of the four stages of non-REM sleep, followed by an episode of REM sleep, usually in that order. A typical sleep cycle takes around 90 minutes to complete and occurs several times during the course of a night. Sleep, dream and repeat.

the stages of sleep

Stage 1

During the first stage of sleep, our brainwaves begin to slow down as we drift from wakefulness into slumber. During this period of relatively light sleep, we can be easily woken up. Our heartbeat, breathing and eye movements slow down and our muscles relax with occasional twitches. These are known as myoclonic jerks and can produce the rather alarming sensation of falling (which fortunately doesn't actually happen). The twitches are caused by the motor areas of the brain being spontaneously stimulated. This first stage of sleep tends to be fairly short, lasting for just a few minutes.

Stage 2

During the second stage of sleep, our heartbeat and breathing continue to slow down and our muscles become even more relaxed. Body temperature drops and eye movements stop. Brain waves, which reflect the activity level of the brain, also become slower, but are interrupted by brief bursts of rapid brain activity called sleep spindles. The second stage of sleep is also the longest, and we spend around half our total sleeping time in this phase.

Stage 3

This is the first stage of deep sleep, when it can become

very difficult to wake someone up. In this stage, brain activity is made up of slow waves known as delta waves, combined with faster waves. If you are woken up during this stage, you are likely to feel groggy and disoriented for a few minutes.

Stage 4

This is the second stage of deep sleep, when brain activity consists almost entirely of delta waves, and breathing and heart rate slow to their lowest levels during sleep. In this stage, it is also very difficult to wake someone up. We need the deep sleep of stages 3 and 4 in order to feel refreshed in the morning, and if these stages are too short, sleep will not feel satisfying.

REM sleep

The final chapter of the sleep cycle generally occurs about 70 to 90 minutes after falling asleep. As the name suggests, REM sleep causes our eyes to move rapidly from side to side, while our eyelids remain closed. In addition, breathing becomes fast, irregular and shallow. Heart rate and blood pressure increase to near waking levels, and the pattern of brain activity is similar to that of someone who is awake and alert. REM sleep is also the stage in which dreaming occurs (although dreams may also occur in non-REM sleep). If you wake up during REM sleep, you can usually vividly recall your dream. It's thought the rapid eye movements are linked to visual images of dreams, although nobody really knows for certain.

Around 20 per cent of total sleep time is composed of REM sleep, but these episodes get longer as the night progresses. So during the first sleep cycle, we spend most of our time in deep sleep, but as the clock ticks towards morning, we spend more time in dream land.

the control centre

Sleep is governed by two biological processes that work together in the brain. The first is our circadian rhythm, aka, the 'body clock'. This is the internally generated rhythm that rises and falls during the day creating the sleep-wake cycle.

If you've slept well, your circadian rhythm will naturally rise in the morning, so you feel awake and alert. It then ebbs and flows through the day, so that many of us feel an urge to sleep between 1pm and 3pm in the afternoon - that 'post lunch slump'. The strongest urge to sleep is usually between 2am and 4am.

Our biological clock is controlled by an area of the brain called the suprachiasmatic nucleus (SCN) in the hypothalamus. The SCN acts as a kind of pacemaker, responding to light and dark. As night falls, the cells of the SCN send a message to the pineal gland, a tiny gland in the brain, to secrete melatonin, the hormone that makes us feel sleepy. Levels of melatonin stay elevated throughout the night encouraging sleep, then decrease as it gets light, promoting wakefulness.

Your circadian rhythm works best when you have a regular sleep pattern, however not everyone's body clock runs to the same time, which is why some people are 'night owls' and some are 'early birds.' A shift in circadian rhythm also occurs during the teenage years. This explains why teenagers tend to want to go to bed later and sleep longer in the morning, resulting in an unfortunate clash with social and educational expectations, through no real fault of the teenager. Our biological clocks also suffer when we change time zones, which is why we experience jetlag after a long-haul flight.

The second part of the sleep 'control centre' is something called 'sleep pressure', which runs alongside our circadian rhythm. This is manifested in the desire to sleep, which becomes increasingly strong as the day progresses. This desire, or pressure, is caused by the build-up of a chemical called adenosine, which is naturally produced in the body. The longer we've been awake, the higher the concentration of adenosine and the more we feel like sleeping. When high levels of adenosine occur at the same time as a dip in circadian rhythm, this creates the perfect moment for sleep. This generally happens in the evening. Then, as we sleep, the concentration of adenosine falls again, resetting sleep pressure for another day. However, as we'll see in chapter 5, this pressure can be temporarily overridden by caffeine and other factors, throwing our sleep pattern into disarray.

the power of a nap

Babies nap throughout the day and toddlers often sleep after lunch. But what about adults? In most modern Western societies, we tend to sleep in one big chunk at night. However, there is some debate as to whether this is natural, and whether we wouldn't be better off having an extended afternoon snooze, much like a Mediterranean siesta. This would tie in with our natural circadian rhythm, and the dreaded slump in energy that is often experienced after lunch.

Unfortunately, most of us don't have the luxury of being able to take a siesta. But studies suggest that even short naps can be beneficial, boosting productivity and alertness, as well as mood. And businesses are beginning to take note, with the arrival of nap rooms and sleep pods. Of course this isn't purely altruistic; a rested workforce is a more efficient one, although there is still a long way to go towards truly flexible, sleep-friendly working hours.

A word of caution though – long, late naps can jeopardise sleep at night, so limit power naps to the early afternoon and keep them short – to a maximum of 30 minutes. Any longer and you risk going too far into your sleep cycle, resulting in a feeling of grogginess, known as sleep inertia. Some research suggests napping for as little as five minutes could be enough to perk us up. However, if you're prone to insomnia, it may be best to skip the nap completely and wait until bedtime.

did you know?

Dreams can vary in length from a few seconds to almost an hour. They tend to last longer as the night progresses.

We can only dream about faces we've already seen, either from television, a photograph, or from a crowd of people, regardless of whether we remember them or not.

50 per cent of a dream is forgotten within five minutes of waking up, and 90 per cent is forgotten within 10 minutes.

REM dreams are often bizarre, while non-REM dreams are repetitive and thought-like, with little imagery.

During REM sleep, your arm and leg muscles become temporarily paralysed. This stops you from acting out your dreams.

We need both REM and non-REM sleep in order to have a good night's sleep.

Newborn babies spend half their total sleep time in REM sleep, but by two years old that is down to only a quarter.

Dreams are the royal road to the unconscious.

SIGMUND FREUD, THE INTERPRETATION OF DREAMS

CHAPTER 3

sleep and the brain

While we are horizontal, all sorts of secret assignments are taking place. In fact, far from being passive, sleep is a time of prolific internal activity.

While we are out for the count, magical things happen inside our brains. Most significant of all is the crucial role that sleep plays in memory and learning.

Whether it's recalling vital facts for an exam, remembering to pick up the kids or to attend a dental appointment, memory oils our everyday lives, helping us to access the information we need and move seamlessly from one thing to another.

We only need to consider the daily struggle of people living with dementia, to realise how difficult it is to function when memory becomes impaired. And on page 29, we'll look at the link between sleep and conditions like Alzheimer's disease.

There is a wealth of evidence to suggest that sleep helps us to remember important information by making room for new memories, and bullet-proofing others so that we don't lose hold of them.

During the day, the brain is bombarded with new information which is held in an area of the brain called the hippocampus. This area acts like a kind a cerebral storage facility. However, the poor put-upon hippocampus can only take in so much at a time – rather like an iCloud that will only let you deposit a certain number of photographs before you need to delete some.

Contrary to the practice of staying up late to revise for exams, studies have shown that humans are significantly better at learning and memorising facts after a full night's sleep. This is due to the remarkable way in which information is shunted from one part of the brain to another while we are unconscious. During sleep, electrical impulses act like a fleet of couriers, transporting data from the hippocampus (the temporary storage facility) to another part of the brain called the cortex, where it can stay more permanently. Not only does this free up space in the hippocampus, restoring the brain's capacity for learning, but it also helps consolidate existing and important information by relocating it to a more stable home.

Studies indicate that this ingenious process happens during those brief bursts of rapid brain activity called sleep spindles which take place during the second stage of sleep. Therefore, if you don't give yourself long enough in bed, you shortchange yourself of spindle-rich sleep, and your ability to learn and remember suffers. In fact, further studies show that even a brief nap can help cement factual information inside our heads.

However, hanging on to all the minutiae of daily life, such as what you ate for dinner last Wednesday, would result in our minds soon becoming clogged up with random, largely redundant bits of information. So while we are asleep, the brain goes a step further and actively sorts the wheat from the chaff, selecting which useful nuggets of knowledge to send to the cortex and which to discard. Like tidying up your desk, or organising your computer files, this makes it easier to retrieve the documents you need without having to wade through all the junk.

Furthermore, sleep doesn't just aid the kind of memory that involves recalling (and forgetting) facts; it also helps with the kind of motor memory needed for acquiring new skills, such as playing sport, or learning a musical instrument.

As strange as this sounds, given that you can't flex your muscles or play the piano when you're unconscious, sleep provides the playing field in which motor skills are transferred to the subconscious. This means they become more instinctive, in the same way as driving a car becomes automatic once you've been doing it for long enough. In fact, many professional sports organisations and coaches are now waking up to the importance of sleep for improved performance. Not only does it boost energy and alertness, it also improves proficiency. Sleep could be the difference between a gold or a bronze, or a win or a lose. Though of course you don't have to be an elite athlete to reap the benefits of staying in bed a bit longer.

However, just as getting enough sleep is great for the mind, not getting enough can have the completely opposite effect. One of the first signs of sleep deprivation is a loss of concentration and reduction in reaction times, and the most dangerous place for this to happen is behind a steering wheel. Drowsy driving is a huge problem on the roads, and causes around one-quarter of all fatal collisions – even more than those caused by drink driving. A microsleep can happen in the blink of an eye without you even realising, with catastrophic consequences. Research shows that sleeping for fewer than seven hours a night impairs cognitive performance, and that the effects get worse the longer it goes on. The science is clear: tiredness kills.

Aside from the obvious physical dangers, poor sleep is also linked to all sorts of mental health conditions including depression and anxiety, and can even increase the risk of having suicidal thoughts. And if you've ever found yourself getting angrier or more upset than usual after a rough night, that's because a lack of sleep can play havoc with our emotions and ability to remain rational. This is because sleep exerts a large influence on the amygdala, the part of the brain concerned with mood, feeling and instinct.

sleep and aging

Poor sleep doesn't just make us feel a bit groggy and grumpy. Persistent and on-going sleep deprivation can also affect mental functioning as well as state of mind. Perhaps most seriously of all, it can even increase the likelihood of developing Alzheimer's disease, the most common form of dementia.

Although poor sleep is a common symptom of Alzheimer's disease, scientists have now discovered that it works both ways, and that people with sleeping problems are at a greater risk of developing the condition in the first place. Studies show that regularly sleeping for fewer than five hours a night in middle age is linked to later cognitive decline, including Alzheimer's disease, due to a clear biological pathway.

Alzheimer's disease is characterised by a build-up of a toxic protein called beta-amyloid which clumps together in the brain to form plaques. Beta-amyloid is present in everyone's brains, and is produced by the activity of neurons. Levels are usually low in the morning and increase during the day. But during the night, this toxic waste product is flushed out while we're at rest. It's as if sleep opens the doors for a band of night-time internal cleaners, who come in to remove the debris of the day.

But in order for this to happen, certain cells in the brain, called glial cells, need to shrink. This creates a kind of drainage system through which the toxic waste can be removed.

However, if sleep is disturbed or cut short, the channels aren't opened up, the waste disposal team can't get in and the clearing process can't happen effectively. The harsh result is a potentially greater risk of developing Alzheimer's disease in the future.

Although this is worrying news for anyone who worries about their sleep, the reverse is also true. By prioritising sleep and putting it on a pedestal along with healthy eating and exercise, we can make a massive difference to our short- and long-term health. This includes reducing the risk Alzheimer's disease by avoiding the build-up of plaque in the brain.

What's more, scientists are currently involved in new exciting research looking at ways of mimicking sleep processes in the brain, to see if they can artificially stimulate ways of flushing out toxic material. This could lead to new ways to treat neurodegenerative diseases and could even offer hope for delaying or preventing the onset of dementia.

did you know?

The amount of sleep you need decreases with age. Older people may only need six or seven hours of sleep a night. As we age, the amount of REM sleep also decreases.

Newborn babies sleep for around 17 hours out of every 24 (unfortunately, not necessarily during the night).

A four-year-old child typically needs around 12 hours of sleep a day. By the age of 10, this falls to around 10 hours a day.

In total, we spend about one-third of our lives asleep. Cats spend around two-thirds of their lives asleep.

At 20 years old, about 20 per cent of our sleep is deep sleep, but for a 70-year-old, it's only 1–2 per cent.

The length of an average night's sleep has dropped from nine hours in the pre-light bulb era to seven-and-a-half hours today.

The best bridge between despair and hope is a good night's sleep.

JOSEPH COSSMAN

CHAPTER 4

sleep and the body

Diet and exercise are widely and loudly flaunted as being the holy grail of good health. But maxing out on cauliflower and avocado while working on those yoga poses – and avoiding stress, sugar, cigarettes and too much alcohol – isn't enough.

At last the world seems to be waking up to the thing your grandmother always told you: 'you'll feel better after a good night's sleep'. It turns out Granny was right. There is now overwhelming evidence that sleep is the most powerful guardian of our health and well-being. We literally can't survive without it.

It's amazing how you can go to bed after a grey and jaded sort of day, but when you get up the following morning (assuming you don't suffer from insomnia) everything seems magically better, as if viewed in a new, sunnier light.

Getting a solid eight hours of sleep doesn't just improve your outlook on life – although that in itself is worth staying in bed for – it can also make a huge difference to your immediate and future health. And while it may not offer total immunity, it does offer proven protection against all sorts of hideous diseases. Better still, sleep is completely free, comes with zero side-effects and is a method that has been tried and tested for centuries. It's also suitable for vegans.

Although your grandparents and their predecessors most likely appreciated the value of rest, it's fair to say that sleep has taken a back seat in more recent times. Thanks to the internet and the blurring of time zones across social media, we now live in an increasingly 24/7 society. Day and night are in danger of losing their identities; we can shop at midnight, talk to someone on the other side of the world in the early hours and answer emails from the bedroom.

The pressure to stay connected means huge swathes of society are sacrificing sleep due to the Fear Of Missing Out. Add to this the escalating demands and competition that many people experience in the workplace, along with the pressure to be all things to all people – to have a successful career while raising a family and maintaining friendships. And in a world where we are so often defined by what we do, often it's our sleep that is the first thing to suffer, both in terms of duration because we're too busy to go to bed, and quality because stress smothers our ability to relax.

Ironically, many people skimp on sleep in order to get things done, but in fact sleep deprivation is a killer of productivity. In some professions there is a culture, even an expectation, of being seen to work late, as a sign of commitment or ambition. Yet there is nothing glamorous or admirable about claiming you can survive on minimal sleep. The simple fact is we cannot live our best life when we're tired. And nowhere is that more apparent than when it comes to our health. Persistent sleep deprivation leaves in its wake a trail of bodily devastation.

Thankfully, things are now turning full circle and sleep is back on the radar again. This is largely due to the emerging and indisputable research showing links between poor sleep and poor health including: high blood pressure, heart disease, diabetes, obesity and even cancer. We are slowly coming round to the idea that we can't survive without sleep.

The best, and perhaps most uncomfortable, way to understand the body's need for sleep is to look at what happens to our physical health when we don't get enough of it. As most people have probably discovered at one time or another, staying up all night causes us to feel fatigued and irritable the next day. And while we can generally make up for one bad night, if sleep deprivation continues, things quickly get worse.

After two nights of no sleep, we become disorientated, lethargic, withdrawn and have trouble concentrating. We struggle to remember things and have difficulty reading and speaking clearly. Body temperature drops, while our appetite surges. After 48 hours of no sleep, we are also much more likely to be impulsive.

On the third day, things reach crisis point. It becomes impossible to think clearly, we lose all grasp of reality and hallucinations take hold. And all this happens after just 72 hours – far less time than it's possible to survive without food.

Obviously, it's impossible, or at least unethical, to perform experiments on humans to see how long we can survive without sleep (thank goodness!) but experiments have been done on rats. These poor creatures, deprived of sleep in the name of science, were dead within three weeks.

Clearly, sleep isn't something to be messed with. But it's not just total sleep deprivation that's the issue; a cumulative loss of sleep over time can also be extremely detrimental. Gradually chipping away at the quality and length of our sleep over many nights or years has long-term health consequences. This is demonstrated by studies looking at the health of shift workers, whose internal biological clocks are unavoidably skewed due to the nature of their jobs. Numerous studies have found higher rates of heart disease, strokes, obesity and cancer in night-shift workers, even when taking into account other lifestyle factors. In fact, the World Health Organization has classified night-shift work as a probable carcinogen due to circadian disruption.

healthy sleep, healthy you

Sleep gives the body a chance to repair muscles and tissues, to replace aging or dead cells and to fight infection. This is because during sleep, the immune system carries out a host of vital regenerative operations that are essential to every biological system in the body.

If you've ever been through a spell of not sleeping well, you may well have found yourself much more susceptible to colds and other minor ailments. That's because when we're deprived of sleep, the immune system doesn't get the chance to defend us against all the common causes of illness. What's more, when we do come down with 'flu, or another infection, all we want to do is stay in bed. This again is the body's way of telling us we need to sleep so that the immune system can get on with its job of making us better.

However, the immune system doesn't merely fight coughs and colds; it also serves the vital function of stalking and destroying much more serious threats including any naturally circulating dangerous cells, which if not exterminated could potentially develop into tumours or cancer. Put simply, a build-up of poor sleep increases the risk of cancer. Of course, the positive side of this is that by doing something as simple as making bedtime a priority, we can reduce our chance of getting this dreadful disease. And not just cancer, but many of the other conditions that plague the 21st century, too.

Besides cancer, one of the major health issues facing modern society is high blood pressure, or hypertension. One in four adults around the world have high blood pressure, which is linked to many serious and potentially life-threatening conditions.

Although it rarely causes symptoms, hypertension is the largest single known risk factor for cardiovascular disease, increasing the risk of heart failure, coronary artery disease and strokes, as well as placing extra strain on other organs, such as the brain, kidneys and eyes. The medical advice is clear: cut down on salt and alcohol, don't smoke, take more exercise, eat healthily and lose weight if necessary. While these are all super important, one lifestyle change is glaringly overlooked. As you've probably guessed by now, it's sleep! It might sound too simple to be true, but research shows that sleep plays a key role in keeping blood pressure in check.

This can be explained by looking at what happens to

blood pressure when we don't sleep. Sleep deprivation causes the sympathetic nervous system to activate the 'fight or flight' response so that we remain in a perpetual state of play. This makes our heart beat faster, causing blood to be pumped more quickly around the body. At the same time, our bodies are subjected to a stream of the stress hormone, cortisol. Unfortunately, cortisol causes blood vessels to constrict, which results in an even greater increase in blood pressure.

To make matters worse, sleep deprivation inhibits the release of another hormone, the growth hormone, which is vital for assisting with repairs around the body, including replenishing the lining of blood vessels – including those which are already under extra strain. On the other hand, deep sleep helps to lower both heart rate and blood pressure, therefore reducing the risk of strokes and other related conditions.

sleep yourself slim

It would be easy to assume that people who sleep more are more likely to be overweight. The good news is, quite the opposite is true! Sleep isn't a measure of laziness; it's a stronghold of health and vitality, and can even help us to maintain a healthy weight. Exhaustion due to a lack of sleep, on the other hand, just leaves us feeling sluggish and is a pretty effective way of keeping us out of the gym. Plus, if you're up half the night, you're more likely to be raiding the fridge.

But middle-of-the-night snacks and a lack of energy to do any exercise aren't the only culprits. Sleep deprivation affects our waistlines at a hormonal level too. If you suffer from insomnia, you may have noticed that you're likely to feel hungrier than normal the next day, or to overeat.

This is because sleep deprivation plays havoc with the hormones that control appetite: namely leptin and ghrelin. Leptin is responsible for telling our brains when we are full, while ghrelin triggers feelings of hunger. Unfortunately, inadequate sleep causes these hormones to become out of kilter – ghrelin levels rise, while leptin levels fall. This results in a double whammy of not knowing when you're full, and feeling the urge to eat even when you don't actually need to.

To make matters worse, when we're tired we're also much more likely to be tempted by sugary treats and quick-fix carbohydrates, rather than healthy meals. And because tiredness also eats away at our willpower and fuels impulsive behaviour, we are more likely to give in to that temptation. It's a lose-lose situation – except when it comes to weight, which is more likely to go in the opposite direction. It's often said that there's no easy way to lose weight. However, improving your sleep pattern could just tip the scales in your favour, without the need for dieting.

Unfortunately, obesity is now a worldwide public health problem, with the percentage of adults and children who are overweight continuing to rise, year on year. Obesity is associated with an increased risk of numerous chronic diseases, including diabetes, heart disease, osteoarthritis and cancer. Poor eating habits and sedentary lifestyles are of course largely to blame, however, given the link between overeating and under sleeping, it stands to reason that sleep may, once again, be a contributing factor.

One of the conditions most likely to develop as a result of obesity is type 2 diabetes. This can occur when glucose levels in the blood become too high. In healthy individuals, insulin instructs the body to remove glucose from the blood, depositing it in cells where it can be used as fuel for energy, or stored for later use. However, if the cells of the body stop responding to insulin, then the ability to absorb glucose from the blood deteriorates. Consequently, blood sugar levels rise and so too does the probability of being diagnosed with type 2 diabetes.

But it's not just what you eat, or how much you eat that can affect your chance of developing the condition. Research shows that sleep can also have a surprising effect on insulin resistance, and a lack of sleep can cause our blood sugar levels to rise. In one study where healthy adults were only allowed to sleep for four or five hours a night for six nights, it was found they were forty percent less able to absorb glucose compared to when they'd had a full night's sleep. A pretty eye-opening result!

Furthermore, research has shown that people who routinely sleep for fewer than six hours a night are far more likely to be diagnosed with type 2 diabetes than those who get an adequate amount of sleep – even when taking into account other lifestyle factors.

Don't fight with the pillow, but lay down your head and kick every worriment out of the bed.

EDMUND VANCE COOKE

did you know?

Growth hormone in children is secreted during sleep, so a child's growth can be stunted by sleep deprivation.

Sleeping for just a few hours rather than a full night lowers your pain threshold.

Humans are the only mammals that willingly delay sleep.

12 per cent of people dream entirely in black and white.

It should take you between 10 and 15 minutes to fall asleep at night. If it takes you fewer than five minutes, this could indicate you are sleep deprived.

The record for the longest period without sleep is 11 days. This was set by 17-year-old Randy Gardner in 1964, and should not be repeated. The Guinness Book of Records no longer recognises attempts, due to the dangers.

Sleep is the best meditation.

DALAI LAMA

CHAPTER 5

beauty sleep and the beasts

As we've already discovered, sleep affects every system and organ in the body. A long, uninterrupted night's slumber is one of the best ways to improve and preserve your health and well-being, and to increase your daytime productivity.

Unfortunately, life has a habit of sabotaging our relationship with sleep, leaving us trapped in a waking nightmare of restless nights and daytime fatigue. Yet by changing old habits, we can end this cycle of poor sleep and start living again.

And Sleep will not
lie down, but walks
Wild-eyed and cries
to Time.

OSCAR WILDE

With the growing pressures of modern living, sleep deprivation and insomnia are becoming increasingly common issues. Insomnia is simply trouble sleeping, and is something almost all of us experience from time to time. Disturbed sleep is often brought about by stressful life events, such as worrying about money, relationships or work, or by life changes such as having children, moving house or starting a new job. For many people, sleep improves once the stressful situation has been resolved. However, for others, the struggle to sleep continues, resulting in chronic insomnia, when despite going to bed at a reasonable hour, sleep refuses to come.

There are two types of insomnia; the first is sleep onset insomnia, which is an inability to fall asleep in the first place. The second is sleep maintenance insomnia, which is trouble staying asleep. It's also possible to suffer from both types of insomnia at the same time.

Insomnia is wretchedly common, with at least one in three people suffering from some degree of sleep loss. However, while it may be common, it's not normal, and given the now well-established link between a lack of sleep and almost every minor and major ailment you can think of, it's a problem that shouldn't be overlooked or dismissed. It's therefore essential to address any underlying issues, and to break the cycle of bad sleeping patterns before damage sets in.

Unfortunately, some of us are just more prone to insomnia than others. This includes women, who are almost twice as likely as men to find it hard to sleep, partly due to those pesky hormones. Pregnancy, motherhood, the menstrual cycle and the menopause can all wreak havoc on our sleeping patterns. In addition, insomnia can sometimes run in families, so having a parent with the condition could increase your chances of following in their footsteps. Other common factors include taking some types of medication, various physical and mental health conditions, as well as getting older.

The good news is, it doesn't matter whether your poor sleep is a result of nature, nurture or both, it is possible to overcome insomnia. And the best place to start is to address any external factors or underlying issues that could be keeping you awake – starting with the obvious one: what you had to drink.

caffeine

At 7 o'clock in the evening, when you're starting to wind down, there's nothing like a nice cup of tea to help you relax. Stop! Step away from the kettle. Subjecting your body to caffeine in the early evening is like inviting your brain to an all-night party, just when you want to turn out the lights.

Caffeine is a chemical that promotes alertness and prevents us from falling asleep. As well as tea and coffee, caffeine is also found in cola, chocolate – especially dark chocolate, energy drinks and some pain relieving tablets and cold remedies. What's more, so-called decaffeinated drinks still contain up to 30 per cent of the amount of caffeine found in regular tea and coffee.

In moderation, and at the right time of day, a stimulating coffee can of course have its advantages. However, while it can take just 30 minutes for the buzz to kick in, the after-effects take far longer to disappear. Caffeine has a half-life of around five hours. This is the length of time it takes for your body to get rid of half the original amount. So if you have a cup of tea or coffee at 7pm, fifty per cent of it will still be swishing around in your metabolism at midnight, and the rest for even longer, which is clearly not conducive to getting a good night's sleep.

At a molecular level, caffeine works by hogging the sleep receptors in your brain. This prevents the sleep-promoting molecule, adenosine, from latching on and doing its job of creating that 'sleep pressure'. So while adenosine is rendered homeless, we are left sleepless and frustrated.

As with any drug, the effects of caffeine vary from person to person, depending on weight, age, genetics and metabolism. Some people are more sensitive to it than others. However, the best advice – especially if you have trouble sleeping – is to set an early curfew and avoid having caffeine during the afternoon, so that most of it is out of your system by the time you go to bed.

stress

If there's one thing guaranteed to come between you and a good night's sleep, it's stress. When you've got a to-do list as long as your duvet, it can be impossible to switch off, and when you do (finally) lie down, physical exhaustion is often no match for worrying about tomorrow.

The problem with stress is that it doesn't just affect our minds, but our bodies too. When we're stressed, this tells the sympathetic nervous system that danger is on the horizon, which activates that 'fight or flight' response. This causes our heart rate to increase, muscles to contract and a surge of adrenalin and other stress hormones to flood our veins - none of which is very helpful when you just want to go to sleep.

A few millennia ago, this response helped our ancestors to fight or run for their lives in the face of real, physical danger. But in the 21st century, it's basically a massive overreaction. The problem is our chimp-brains still haven't worked this out, so any kind of stress, whether it's a prowling lion or a bulging inbox, results in the same physiological response. And when we feel stressed on a daily basis, this can cause us to live in a perpetual state of heightened awareness and anxiety, leading to chronic insomnia.

On the positive side, while we can't always eliminate the source of stress, we can change how we react to it, through things like cognitive behavioural therapy, mindfulness, hypnotherapy, breathing exercises and relaxation techniques, some of which we'll look at in the next chapter. By changing our response to stress, we can also reset our ability to sleep.

the tech effect

There's no doubt that technology has revolutionised the world; we are better connected and more informed than ever before. But technology also dominates our lives and wrecks our sleep. Homes and bedrooms are filled with things that flash, beep, buzz and shine all night long, begging for attention. Scores of people lie in bed obsessively, compulsively checking emails or trawling through social media, instead of reading a good book – or even going to sleep.

Studies have also found that the blue LED light emitted by electronic devices like smartphones, tablets and e-readers can suppress the production of melatonin, the hormone that helps us to maintain a steady circadian rhythm. When this happens, the body and brain miss their normal cues to wind down and prepare for sleep. One study found that people who used an e-reader before bedtime took longer to fall asleep, had less REM sleep and were more tired when woken after eight hours compared to people who read a printed book before going to sleep. Computers and TVs also produce blue light, but as we tend to sit further away from them, the dosage isn't as high. Yet there's no getting away from the fact that digital screens and insomnia are partners in crime. The unequivocal advice is to switch them off an hour before bedtime (and dim the brightness settings during the evening) and ideally, keep them out of the bedroom.

alcohol

Alcohol is often considered to be an aid to sleep, whereas in fact it's nothing of the sort. Drinking in the evening can cause arousal during the night, making you wake up repeatedly – and not just because you need to use the bathroom.

Although alcohol is a sedative, sedation and sleep aren't the same thing at all.

Enjoying a few glasses of wine might cause you to crash out quickly once you hit the pillow (possibly in some degree of drunken stupor) but it also disrupts the brain's normal patterns of sleep. This can lead to fragmented sleep peppered with awakenings, leaving you feeling groggy and unrefreshed in the morning, irrespective of any hangover. Furthermore, alcohol suppresses the brain's ability to generate REM sleep, which is also when we dream the most. This kind of sleep helps us maintain emotional stability, and is when our brain sorts through memories and experiences, so missing out on dream sleep, especially on a regular basis, can be extremely detrimental to these processes.

Obviously, there will be holidays and exceptions, but as a rule, it's best to have no more than one or two drinks a day, and no later than three hours before bedtime. It might sound dull, but you'll feel a whole lot brighter.

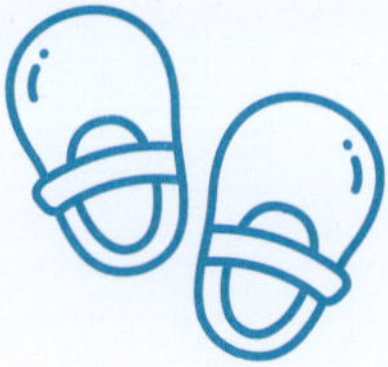

the patter of tiny feet

As any parent will testify, nothing is more likely to sabotage your sleep pattern than a new baby. Research suggests that the average parent loses more than a full month's sleep in the first year of having a baby. And of course, the added irony is that you have never been more tired. Unfortunately, babies arrive in the world with very little concept of day and night, which can leave parents in a weird state of jet lag. While some postnatal sleep deprivation is inevitable, getting babies into a very basic evening routine before putting them down to sleep can help you all to adjust. When sleep deprivation is unavoidable, it's essential to make self-care a priority, so take a power nap, meditate for five minutes and don't stress over household chores. Most importantly, it's worth remembering that the gruelling nights do come to an end, and that night and day will return.

did you know?

Research shows we sleep better during a new moon and worse during a full moon, though the reason for this is something of a mystery.

Dysania is the term used to describe an inability to get out of bed in the morning.

Humans can sleep with their eyes open.

Deaf people commonly sign while sleeping.

It's harder to sleep at high altitudes due to the reduced amount of oxygen.

You can't sneeze while sleeping.

People in the Netherlands are thought to get the most sleep, with an average of eight hours and five minutes per night, while people in Singapore get the least, with an average of seven hours and twenty-four minutes per night.

It is a common experience that a problem difficult at night is resolved in the morning after the committee of sleep has worked on it.

JOHN STEINBECK

CHAPTER 6

defeating the beasts:

how to improve your sleep

So, you've cut the caffeine, tackled areas of stress, given up the nightcap and banished screens from the bedroom. But you still can't sleep! It's time to make some lifestyle changes and to examine your sleep hygiene.

Despite the way it sounds, sleep hygiene has nothing to do with changing your sheets or washing your pillow cases (although fresh bedding is always nice), and involves transforming your sleeping environment from a battleground into a bed of roses (minus the thorns, of course). It's time to take sleep-action!

A ruffled mind makes a restless pillow.

CHARLOTTE BRONTE

Some people are blessed with an uncanny ability to fall asleep just minutes after closing their eyes, regardless of what kind of chaos is going on around them. Such people are usually either toddlers, or just extremely fortunate (and unusual) individuals. For the rest of us, it helps to have somewhere that's inviting, comfortable and restful in which to lie down, somewhere that is our own little sanctuary. This doesn't mean splashing out on silk sheets, ambient lighting, or designer pyjamas; all you need is a comfortable mattress (most need replacing after ten years) and somewhere that's cool, dark and quiet. Oh, and remember, the bedroom is purely for sleeping (and sex) and should never be used for work, arguments or filling out tax returns. So how do you create the perfect sleeping environment?

temperature

Resist the urge to ramp up the heating at night. A room that's too hot can seriously hamper your chances of getting a good night's sleep. That's because body temperature peaks in the evening and then drops to its lowest levels when you're asleep. You can help with this process by taking a warm bath before bed; the hot water increases your body temperature, and the cooling-off period that follows mimics the natural drop that happens at night, helping you to become drowsy. There's no need to create an ice-chamber though – an ideal bedroom temperature is around 16–18°C (60–65°F) although young children and elderly people may need it slightly higher. It's also a good idea to have different bedding for different seasons.

sound

There's nothing quite like raucous neighbours or a barking dog to prevent you from getting a sound night's sleep. Or worse, sleeping next to a snorer. Of course, external noise isn't always easy to control, especially if you live in an inner city or a large apartment block. However, there are measures you can take to block out unwanted sounds, including double glazing, ear plugs and white noise tapes. And if your partner snores, you might want to suggest a trip to the doctor (or the spare room).

light

There's a reason we sleep when it's dark. It's because darkness causes our bodies to release melatonin, which helps us to drift off. Daylight, on the other hand, signals to our bodies that it's time to wake up and get cracking. This explains why many of us have a hard time sleeping during the summer. To create an illusion of night time, it's worth investing in some heavy curtains, or blackout blinds. Alternatively, you could try using an eye mask. And of course, keep those blue light-emitting screens well out of sight.

get some rays

Natural light is crucial to keeping your internal clock ticking, promoting healthy sleep. So exposure to bright light during the day can help you to sleep at night. Try to get outdoors first thing in the morning, and take a break during the day, too. Although outdoor sunlight is best, bright indoor light can be beneficial as well. So if you really can't get outside, try sitting or standing near a window. If you work in an office or from home, move your desk to where it will receive the most light. If that's not possible, studies have shown that indoor lighting, from bright lamps or phototherapy lamps during the day, can also help.

move it

Regular activity is good – not just for physical and mental health, happiness and a sense of well-being – but for sleep, too. Exercise can help tire you out and relax your body, helping you to fall asleep faster and more soundly. But doing too much strenuous activity too close to bedtime can have the reverse effect. Exercise stimulates the body to secrete the stress hormone cortisol, which helps activate the alerting mechanism in the brain, so the post-workout high can prevent you from nodding off. So while exercise is undoubtedly beneficial, save the bootcamp for when you get up, and try not to exercise any closer than three hours before you go to bed.

stick to a routine

A sleep-friendly routine doesn't start half an hour, or even an hour, before bedtime; it starts 16 hours before bedtime! It starts by getting up at the same time each day and going to bed at the same time each evening. It might sound dull and predictable, but regularity really is key when it comes to sleep – and that means sticking to the same timetable, morning and night. And yes, that includes weekends! Of course, if you've had a late night, the temptation is to binge-sleep the following morning. Unfortunately, doing so messes up your circadian rhythm – the cycle that controls when you're awake and when your body is ready for sleep – making it harder to sleep the next night. Waking up at the same time each day is the best way to set your internal clock, so try to limit lie-ins to a maximum of one hour. Even if you didn't sleep well the night before, the extra sleep pressure will help you consolidate sleep the following night.

It can also help to have a few other regular habits before turning out the lights. These might include having a bath, reading a book (a paperback not an e-Reader) burning some relaxing lavender or other aromatherapy oil, having a soothing drink and writing down any worries or things you need to remember the following day in a journal so that you don't take them to bed with you. As well as helping you to relax, these things signal to your body that it will soon be time to sleep.

relax

If after resetting the thermostat, eliminating every last wisp of light and whisper of noise, and sticking to a routine like Velcro, you're still tossing and turning, then it's time to delve deeper.

Because sleep hygiene is only part of the story. Making sure your sleeping environment is cool, dark and comfortable is great, but it's futile if you ignore the internal issues that are preventing you from getting to sleep; the troublesome thoughts, the endless worries, the over-active mind.

In the small hours of the night, the ultimate nemesis of sleep is stress. Or more specifically, the way we deal with stress. Because at 4am there is probably very little you can do about whatever situation is bothering you, other than let it go and relax.

Of course, just telling yourself to relax is unlikely to have any effect, especially if you have an active mind. The key is to retrain your mind to calm down, and this is where things like mindfulness and meditation can be extremely beneficial. Some people also find apps like Headspace and Calm to be helpful.

Another powerful aid to relaxation is visualisation. This works by calling on the imagination to conjure up calming images, gently drawing the mind away from negative thoughts and worries. It's also a lot less boring than counting sheep. Try using the following simple outline, or invent one of your own.

calming visualisation exercise

Close your eyes and take yourself to a beautiful, relaxing place. Perhaps a soothing forest or meadow full of wild flowers. Or imagine a wonderful beach.

•

You're lying on soft, golden sand beneath an unbroken, blue sky.

•

Hear the sounds of the softly crashing waves, smell the salt in the air, feel the sand against your skin.

•

Imagine it in as much detail as you can, letting all your senses become involved. Really make the place come alive.

•

As you conjure up this place in your mind, allow the tension in your forehead and around your jaw and neck to dissolve.

•

Become aware of your breath slowing down and going right down into your belly.

•

Try to remain immersed in your imaginary place until you feel yourself drifting off to sleep.

Although you might get distracted at first, try to practise visualisation every night. If your mind wanders, just bring it back to your special place. In time, you should find that by distracting your mind from intrusive thoughts, it becomes easier and easier to relax, and going to this beautiful place signals to your brain that it's time for sleep.

and breathe

You might not think of your lungs as being connected to your state of mind, but the way we breathe sends a clear message to the nervous system, which helps determine whether we feel on edge or at ease. And since stress is such a notorious nocturnal thief, it follows that if we can lower our stress levels through the power of our breath, we will outdo one of the biggest enemies of sleep.

Yet most of the time, we don't give our breath so much as a fleeting thought. When we're anxious or under pressure, our breathing naturally becomes faster and shallower. This sets off biological alarm bells in the brain, causing the sympathetic nervous system to trigger the 'fight or flight' response. This leads to a rise in heart rate, blood pressure and stress hormones, which can be useful if you're fighting off an attacker, but much less so if you want to get to sleep.

Yet by learning to consciously control our breath, we can switch off the 'fight or flight' response and engage the parasympathetic nervous system instead. This is the part of the nervous system that helps us to chill out by triggering the release of calming hormones that tell the body to rest and digest.

Amazingly, we can bring about this relaxed state simply by changing the way we breathe. The important thing is to breathe into the tummy, rather than the chest. This is called abdominal breathing or belly breathing. As well as having a positive impact on your mental and physical health, abdominal breathing can also provide an antidote to insomnia.

You can practise abdominal breathing anywhere, but if you're using it for sleep purposes it makes sense to do it in bed. Start by lying on your back and simply notice the pattern of your breath as you inhale and exhale. Then place one hand on your upper chest, and one hand on your abdomen just below your rib cage. Relax your shoulders and hands. Breathe in through your nose and allow your abdomen to rise; your chest should stay fairly still. Then breathe out through your mouth, noticing how your abdomen flattens as you exhale.

Once you feel comfortable with abdominal breathing, try the following calming breath technique to engage the parasympathetic nervous system and help calm the body. It involves breathing in through the nose, holding the breath, then making an audible whooshing noise with the mouth. The exhale needs to be twice as long as the inhale.

•

Breathe in deeply through your nose for a count of four, expanding your belly on the in-breath.

•

Hold your breath for a count of seven.

•

Exhale through your mouth for a count of eight while making a soft whooshing sound. If it helps, purse your lips and imagine that you are slowly blowing out a candle. This is one breath.

•

Inhale again and repeat the cycle a few more times.

•

You will notice that after a while your body and mind begin to feel calmer.

Don't worry about how slowly or quickly you count; the important thing is to maintain an even pace and to keep the 4:7:8 ratio. If you find it difficult to start with, speed the whole exercise up. With practice, you can slow it down and get used to inhaling and exhaling more and more deeply. Try to practise this exercise before going to sleep each night and at other times during the day. After a few weeks, you should notice a difference.

Let her sleep, for when she wakes she will move mountains.

UNKNOWN

on the menu

Tucking into a large, spicy curry at 10 o'clock at night could be a recipe for insomnia, not to mention indigestion. As well as leaving you with an uncomfortably full stomach, eating too close to bedtime means your body will be focusing on digesting rather than sleeping. This can also cause an increase in body heat, challenging the natural drop in body temperature that happens during sleep. Fatty and spicy foods can also lead to heartburn, further hampering your chances of nodding off.

For a comfortable night's sleep, it's best to leave at least three hours between eating and going to bed, and to stick to fairly light meals, especially if you have a sensitive stomach. And don't forget to lay off the alcohol and caffeine. Remember, these can occur in foods as well as drinks; tiramisu for example – which translates as 'pick me up' – is not really the effect you should be aiming for in the pursuit of sleep.

However, while it makes sense to avoid huge platefuls of rich food close to bedtime, there are some foods that are thought to have a somniferous effect. These include foods that increase the levels of natural compounds that send sleep signals to your brain. And while it's unlikely that any single food will provide a magical panacea for insomnia, snacking on some of the following suggestions, in conjunction with a sleep-healthy lifestyle, may just nudge you towards a more restful night.

cherries

You might not think of fruit as being the most obvious choice for a bedtime snack, but tart cherries are one of the best sources of naturally occurring melatonin – the hormone that helps to regulate your sleep-wake cycle. In fact, in one trial, participants who drank tart cherry juice concentrate were found to have significantly higher levels of melatonin in their bodies after just one week. This was linked to a higher total sleep time and better sleep efficiency. Other direct sources of melatonin include dried cherries, walnuts, rolled oats, oranges and pineapple. In reality, if you are planning on eating rather than drinking cherries, you would probably need an awful lot of them to produce any kind of soporific effect. Although, on the plus side, they are packed full of antioxidants and plenty of other health-promoting substances.

almonds

As well as being a great source of healthy fats, almonds are rich in magnesium, the mineral known as 'nature's tranquiliser'. Magnesium has been shown to improve sleep quality due to its effect on calming the nervous system and relaxing the muscles. Studies have shown that even a small lack of magnesium can lead to disturbed sleep, and a deficiency may even lead to restless leg syndrome, which can severely affect sleep. Besides almonds, other magnesium-rich foods include pumpkin and sunflower seeds, bananas, fish and leafy green vegetables, or you could take a supplement. Epsom salt also contains magnesium, and can be added to the bath as the mineral can be absorbed through the skin.

warm milk

Having a bedtime drink of milk may be more than just an old wife's tale or a childhood ritual, and may actually help you get to sleep thanks to the high levels of both tryptophan and calcium. As well as being good for bones, calcium is another mineral that helps the brain make melatonin. Other good sources of calcium include other dairy products, leafy greens, soya beans, tofu, nuts and sardines.

bananas

Cheap, nutritious and readily available, bananas contain a package of sleep-promoting substances. These include magnesium and potassium, which work together to encourage relaxation and restful sleep. Bananas are also a source of sleep-promoting tryptophan and vitamin B6. As well as playing a role in the production of serotonin and melatonin, vitamin B6 is thought to appease anxiety, and a deficiency in this essential vitamin has been linked to symptoms of depression, which can also be linked to insomnia.

turkey (but not too much)

Turkey is a famously good source of tryptophan, an amino acid that is thought to increase levels of melatonin and serotonin. While melatonin helps govern your internal clock, serotonin can help lift your mood, which can also influence sleep. However, as turkey is high in protein, eating too much of it could cancel out the effect. This is because high levels of protein compete with tryptophan, blocking it from getting into the brain. So keep portions small and include other sources of tryptophan too, such as almonds, dairy, chickpeas, nuts and seeds.

chamomile tea

Drinking a cup of chamomile tea has long been promoted as a natural sleeping aid, although it's not actually a tea, but a herbal infusion made from dried flowers. As well as providing a relaxing ritual, chamomile is a rich source of plant compounds called apigenins. These bind to certain receptors in the brain, reducing anxiety and acting as a mild sedative, helping you to feel soothed and sleepy. For maximum effect, use at least two tea bags and let them stew for a while. If chamomile isn't your cup of tea, then passion flower tea can also help promote relaxation, and research suggests it can help you sleep more soundly. This is thought to be due to the presence of Harman alkaloids – chemicals that calm the nervous system, resulting in a more relaxed sleep.

white rice

While brown rice is usually considered to be the healthier option, white rice may be a better choice if you have trouble sleeping. This is because white rice has a high GI, or Glycaemic Index – the rate at which a food breaks down into sugars in the bloodstream. This means that white rice creates a large spike in blood sugar. This triggers a surge of insulin, which drives the amino acid tryptophan into the brain where it is converted into serotonin, helping to trigger sleep. One study found that people who ate jasmine rice within four hours of going to bed enjoyed significantly better sleep than those who ate other types of rice.

oats

Although more typically eaten for breakfast, oats could make the perfect pre-sleep snack due to the combination of complex carbohydrates, B vitamins and tryptophan. Although tryptophan can be obtained from a variety of foods, research suggests that the brain can convert it into serotonin most easily when it comes from foods that are rich in carbohydrates. So not only do oats provide the tryptophan, but they also help the brain convert it. And despite the recent low-carb trend, when it comes to sleep, carbohydrates are thought to make you sleepy while protein makes you more alert.

And the night shall be
filled with music,
And the cares, that
infest the day,
Shall fold their tents
like the Arabs,
and silently steal away.

HENRY WADSWORTH LONGFELLOW

CHAPTER 7

weird, wonderful and wise:

the Zzzz list of sleep hacks

From listening to random people on the internet brushing their hair – yes, really – to inviting the power of nature into your bedroom, to repainting the walls and getting rid of junk, this section explores some of the many tricks and techniques that are believed to help lull us to sleep, and looks at the science behind the claims. So close the curtains, turn out the lights and snuggle up with a good book, some lavender oil and a few potted plants. Sleep has never looked so inviting.

tidy up!

Are you constantly losing a slipper, or tripping over the jumble of shoes at the foot of your bed? Do you have a 'laundry chair' stacked with clothing that exists in a permanent state of limbo between the wardrobe and the washing machine? Are your drawers groaning with so many 'favourite' tops, that you can never find the one you want? Most of us have way more clothes and possessions than we actually need. As well as taking up physical space, having oodles of stuff around can also take up mental space, which is why decluttering – especially in the bedroom – can help create a calmer, more sleep-friendly environment.

Tidying up is an emotional as well as physical process which helps us to decide what's really important, as well as making it easier to find things. It encourages us to appreciate what we have, while teaching us to be more mindful of our purchases. So refrain from investing in storage solutions, which simply encourage us to hoard in a tidier way, and concentrate on keeping the things you really value or need, and giving away or recycling the things you don't. A clean and minimalist sleeping space is far more conducive to rest and relaxation than one that resembles a child's playroom, or the aftermath of a student house party. So if you only tidy one room in your home, make it your bedroom.

add colour

Once you've cleared the floor and emptied the wardrobe, why not tackle the walls? The colour of a room doesn't just reflect our personality and preferences; it can also set the atmosphere, influencing our mood and state of mind. To create a relaxing, sleep-inducing environment, don't worry about the latest colour trends – which come and go anyway – and stick to sedative shades. Cooler hues like greys, blues and purples have been shown to reduce stress and anxiety, and blue is said to bring down blood pressure and heart rate, while calming the breath. Likewise, delicate shades of purple, such as lavender and lilac, can help bring about a restful quality, contributing to a serene and relaxing sleeping space. On the other hand, loud vibrant colours like red and orange are considered to be stimulating and energising, which isn't ideal if you want to get to sleep. So if these are your favourites, save them for another part of the house. If you don't have time for painting and decorating, or are living in a rented magnolia property where paintbrushes are off-limits, then why not release your inner interior designer with fabrics and soft furnishings? Cushions and throws can add a relaxing spa-like vibe to any room, or you could treat yourself to some new bedding in soothing shades of blue and grey to give your sleeping space that extra sense of tranquillity.

rock-a-bye

Babies have been rocked to sleep for generations, and now science suggests that adults could benefit, too. In one study, researchers from the University of Geneva built a special bed that rocked gently throughout the night. They found that people who took part in the study fell asleep faster and slept more deeply in the rocking bed, as compared to a regular bed. It's thought the rhythmic swinging motion works on the brain, resulting in a longer period of the slow brainwaves associated with deep sleep. What's more, deep sleep is known to play an important role in memory consolidation, and researchers also found that the participants who had been rocked during sleep performed better in memory tests the following day, than those who hadn't. Unfortunately, adult-sized rocking beds have yet to make an appearance in flat-pack furniture stores, so your best bet is probably a hammock.

curl up with a book

The bedtime story is a simple, time-honoured ritual and one that we need to cling on to for all sorts of reasons. Many people swear a good book helps them to nod off, and science backs this up. One study found that just six minutes of reading reduced stress by up to 68 per cent. This is because reading distracts the mind, providing a form of escapism free from day-to-day worries. And unlike television, films and screens, books are silent and relaxing, and don't emit blue light. Getting lost in a book also causes our muscles to relax and our breathing to slow down, instilling a sense of calm in preparation for a good night's sleep. But as well as promoting relaxation, reading broadens the mind, boosting knowledge, creativity, empathy and even lowering the risk of Alzheimer's disease. So whether you struggle to sleep or not, reading a chapter in bed is a habit that shouldn't be consigned to childhood. Although if you are hoping to drop off after a few pages, you might want to avoid anything that's overly scary or exciting. War and Peace, anyone?

do a brain dump

When life is full to the brim, it's easy to lie in bed mentally running over the 235 things you have to do tomorrow. Obviously this isn't going to help you sleep – just as it isn't going to help you achieve any of the jobs on your to-do list. But one thing you can do is to write it all down. Putting tasks to paper can help get them out of your head and diminish the fear of forgetting something. This in turn can help you to feel a little more at ease and in control, so you can stop worrying about tomorrow and sleep.

As well as just making lists of everything you need to do, why not make a gratitude list, too? Keep a journal next to your bed and every night before turning out the light, write down three things that happened that day for which you are thankful. They don't have to be huge, it's important to enjoy small moments too, and to appreciate the things we sometimes take for granted, such as the sun shining, or catching up with a friend, going for a walk, or simply being in good health. Research shows that people who practise gratitude tend to experience greater life satisfaction and less depression than those who don't, and a positive frame of mind is a great asset for a good night's sleep.

imagine you're in Provence

Loved by grandmothers, lavender is probably the most well-known sleep aid of all. Yet the long-held belief in the magical properties of this flowering plant is more than just ancient wisdom – it's also a matter of biochemistry. If you have ever wondered why scents can have such a powerful hold over us, sometimes triggering a vivid memory, or evoking a particular place or person, it's because our sense of smell is linked directly to the limbic system – the part of our brain involved with behavioural and emotional responses. This complex area of the brain is also responsible for controlling the autonomic nervous system, which governs things like heart rate, blood pressure and breathing. So when we inhale the aromatic molecules contained within essential oils, this triggers a series of reactions in the body, activating neurotransmitters, or chemical messengers like serotonin, endorphins and noradrenalin which in turn influence pulse, breathing, blood pressure and many other functions. While some oils can be stimulating, others like lavender can be deeply calming, and there are many studies showing the power of lavender oil to help relieve stress and promote better sleep. So place a few drops in a diffuser, or rub some body oil onto your skin and imagine you're drifting away in the lavender fields of Provence.

listen to strange noises

Still awake? How about listening to someone whispering into a microphone, or turning pages in a book, or even brushing their hair? One of the more bizarre methods of inducing sleep is ASMR, or autonomous sensory meridian response. Commonly described as a brain-tingling, it's a sedative sensation some people experience as a result of certain sights and sounds, like whispers, taps and crackles. The feeling is characterised by the tingling of the skin that starts at the crown of the head and travels down the spine, leading to an increased sense of calm. As weird as it sounds, it's a hugely growing trend, and ASMR videos on YouTube have been viewed millions of times. The craze has attracted the attention of scientists too, and research suggests that ASMR can have the same benefits as relaxation techniques like mindfulness.

reset your circadian rhythm

Sometimes, you need to make things worse in order to make them better. One way to do this can be to drastically restrict the amount of time you spend in bed. The idea is to go to bed at 1am and get up at 6am every day for two weeks. Resist the urge to go to bed any earlier, or to get up later – regardless of how many of those five hours you've actually slept for. Although it sounds extreme, or even counter-productive, stick to this regime for two weeks and don't allow yourself to nap during the day.

It's a challenging technique and probably not one to try if you have a lot of other things going on in your life at the same time. However, some experts believe that restricting the window of sleep can reset your natural ability to sleep. And if you can't sleep anyway, you've got nothing to lose. Gradually, you should start to sleep more during that five-hour window. When this happens, you can start going to bed a little earlier and getting up a little later each day, until you end up with a more normal sleep routine.

don't just lie there

As any occasional or long-suffering insomniac will know, there's nothing worse than lying there physically and mentally exhausted, yet unable to drop off. You toss and turn, flip the pillow, count imaginary sheep or recite poetry in your head, yet nothing works. You watch the minutes tick by with a rising sense of desperation that turns to panic as you count how many hours are left until you need to face the day, and realise it's not nearly enough.

Perhaps you watch your partner slumbering soundly beside you and are filled with an uncharacteristic sense of anger or resentment. As their breath rises and falls with the sound of sleep, you are overcome with an unreasonable urge to wake them so they can share your pain, your frustration. Why can other people sleep, when you can't? What do they have that you don't? If only you could find the remote control for your brain. If only you didn't have to get up in the morning. The most frustrating thing about striving for sleep is that the harder you try, the more unlikely it becomes. What's more, lying in bed awake can actually make insomnia worse by training the mind and body to associate your bed with stress rather than sleep. So if after 30 minutes you are still awake, becoming increasingly tense or despondent, get up and do something else. Read a magazine, have a bowl of cereal, do some stretches, listen to music or do something useful that's not too stimulating, such as sorting out the washing or making packed lunches. At least you will be productive instead of wasting time not sleeping. And by chilling out for a bit, you will be more likely to sleep when you do return to bed.

remember you're not alone

In the unforgiving hours of darkness, suspended between night and day, insomnia can feel like the loneliest place on earth, a purgatory with neither moon nor sun. So it might help to think about all the other sufferers out there who are feeling just like you. Insomnia is a deeply personal and alienating experience, but at the same time it's one that is experienced by hundreds of thousands, if not millions of people all over the world. And while this yawning acknowledgement might not help you to sleep, it may help you to feel less alone.

embrace the power of plants

You might not think of a bedroom as being the obvious place to exercise your green fingers, but many plants have wonderful relaxing and purifying properties. In the late 1980s, NASA did a Clean Air Study, which found that a number of indoor plants were highly effective at removing toxic chemicals from our surroundings. These included substances like benzene, formaldehyde, trichloroethylene, xylene and ammonia, which have been linked to headaches, dizziness, eye irritation and other ailments. By filtering out these chemicals and replacing them with oxygen, plants can help improve air quality, which can in turn promote better health and sleep. The Clean Air Study suggests we should place at least one plant in every hundred square feet of our home or office space, and although it was done some time ago, it's still regarded as a seminal piece of research, and the findings have been backed up by other studies.

As well as helping to clean the air, adorning our homes with flowers and foliage has many psychological benefits, too. Plants, whether indoor or outdoor, help us to feel more in touch with the living world, and there are numerous studies to show that an increased sense of connection to nature plays a key role in alleviating stress and anxiety, which are of course both leading causes of insomnia. So don't worry if you don't know your Spathiphyllum from your Hedera Helix, the following plants all make perfect bedside companions, and are (almost!) impossible to kill. They will also provide a beautiful design feature.

Peace lily

The name alone is almost enough to send you to sleep, but peace lilies are another top air purifier. They also boost indoor humidity, which can make for a more peaceful night by easing dry throats or sinus problems that can disturb your sleep. This lovely plant, which produces white flowers, will flourish in the bedroom as it thrives in shade and only needs watering about once a week.

English ivy

As well as absorbing toxic chemicals from the air, this trailing plant has been shown to improve symptoms of allergies or asthma – both of which can affect quantity and quality of sleep. In one study, The American College of Allergy, Asthma & Immunology found that English Ivy removed 94 per cent of airborne faeces and 78 per cent of airborne mould in just twelve hours. What's more, it's beautifully low-maintenance and will happily put up with cool temperatures and a shady environment. Place it on a shelf or an indoor hanging basket and let it trail down. Just keep it out reach of children and pets, as it's toxic.

Valerian

Unlike the previous plants, this one hasn't been studied for its air purifying abilities, but for its sleep-inducing scent. And while the effects are unlikely to be very powerful, there is some evidence to suggest that the sweetly scented pink or white flowers can improve the quality and quantity of sleep. Failing that, at least you'll have a pleasantly fragranced bedroom. Meanwhile, the dried rhizome and roots are sometimes used in supplements or herbal teas. When kept indoors, valerian is best placed on a sunny windowsill as it needs plenty of light.

Spider plant

It might sound like an arachnophobic nightmare, but spider plants don't actually attract spiders. The name comes from the 'spidery' babies that grow at the end of the long stems. This common house plant is another welcome addition to the bedroom due to its air cleansing abilities. The NASA study showed it removed around 90 per cent of the potentially cancer-causing chemical formaldehyde from the air, which is commonly found in building materials and household products like adhesives, grout and fillers. Spider plants also absorb unpleasant odours and fumes, helping to create a more sleep-inducing atmosphere. Fast-growing and easy to care for, all you have to do is remember to water it occasionally.

Aloe Vera

This popular succulent plant has been used in medicine for centuries, and the gel from the leaves can be used to treat all sorts of conditions from minor cuts and burns to insect bites, dry skin and acne. It also ranked highly in NASA's Clean Air Study, so will help to purify your bedroom too, making for a more restful night. Known as the 'plant of immortality' by the Egyptians, it reproduces freely, so you'll soon have enough for every room in the house. Aloe Vera is easy to care for and will do best on a sunny windowsill. Simply water it about once every three weeks when it becomes dry, and don't allow it to stand in water.

Snake plant

Also known as Mother-in-law's tongue, this is one of the best plants of all for improving indoor air quality. It's known to absorb a number of hazardous chemicals, leaving your bedroom air cleaner. At the same time, this popular plant takes in carbon dioxide while releasing oxygen throughout the night. Like other bedroom-friendly plants, it requires little more than watering every two or three weeks.

My relationship to plants becomes closer and closer. They make me quiet; I like to be in their company.

PETER ZUMTHOR

and finally

In an ideal world, sleep should descend effortlessly and easily, as reliably as the sun sinks beneath the horizon at the end of each day. When this doesn't happen, we tend to try too hard, and sleep slips even further out of reach. This makes us miserable and stressed, which only perpetuates the cycle of anxiety and insomnia. In the unyielding hours of the night, slumber can feel more like a Sisyphean battle than a gentle act of nature.

There are of course times when it's a good idea to see your doctor, or a sleep specialist, especially if your insomnia has been going on for some time and is causing you distress. But remember, everyone is born with the ability to sleep; we are all biologically programmed to drift off and dream. Sometimes it's just a question of rewiring the switch.

So if you have tried every trick in the book and every

technique under the moon and are still struggling to sleep, the best thing to do can be to take a step back and do absolutely nothing. Although this seems counter productive, the most infuriating thing about insomnia is that the harder you try to beat it, the less likely you are to succeed.

In fact, ask someone who sleeps well what they do to get a good night's sleep and they will probably tell you that they just get into bed and turn out the light. Lucky them. For the rest of us for whom sleep doesn't come so placidly, sometimes we simply need to stop reaching for the stars. By reducing the effort in the short term, you will be more likely to succeed in the long term. Because when you step away from the problem, you also step away from the anxiety surrounding the problem, and that in itself may be half the battle.

Sometimes, we just need to let go and stop focusing on sleep as something that is separate from the rest of our lives. Just as we have seen how sleep doesn't happen in isolation from the brain and body, it doesn't happen in isolation from the rest of our existence either. In essence and in nature, sleep is just the closing act of every day; no more, no less.

The best sleep therefore stems from taking a holistic approach to life. Because it isn't just about what you do when you go to bed; it's about everything you do when you are awake too. Sleep can be the tax you pay, or the reward you reap. Remember, if you live well you will sleep well, and if you sleep well, you will live well.

Even a soul submerged in sleep is hard at work and helps make something of the world.

HERACLITUS